Thematic Poetry

On the Farm

More Than 30 Perfect Poems with Instant Activities to Enrich
Your Lessons, Build Literacy, and Celebrate the Joy of Poetry

by Betsy Franco and Friends

SCHOLASTIC
PROFESSIONAL BOOKS

New York • Toronto • London • Auckland • Sydney • Mexico City • New Delhi • Hong Kong

For Maria Damon,
who gives me confidence in my poetry

I would especially like to thank Marcy Barack, Stephanie
Calmenson, Patricia Hubbell, Joy N. Hulme, Sandra Liatsos,
Kris Aro McLeod, Robert Scotellaro, and Katie McAllaster
Weaver who helped make this collection come alive. I am also
very grateful for Liza Charlesworth, my wonderful editor.

ACKNOWLEDGMENTS

MARCY BARACK. "Chores" by Marcy Barack. Copyright © 2000 by Marcy Barack. Used by permission of Marian Reiner for the author.

SO-CHING BRAZER. "Pretty Little Rooster" translated and adapted by Betsy Franco and So-Ching Brazer. Copyright © 2000 by Betsy Franco and So-Ching Brazer. Used by permission of the authors.

GWENDOLYN BROOKS. "Rudolph Is Tired of the City" from BRONZEVILLE BOYS AND GIRLS by Gwendolyn Brooks. Copyright © 1956 by Gwendolyn Brooks Blakely. Used by permission of HarperCollins Publishers.

STEPHANIE CALMENSON. "Barnyard Chat" by Stephanie Calmenson. Copyright © 2000 by Stephanie Calmenson. Used by permission of Marian Reiner for the author.

AILEEN FISHER. "Baby Chick" from RUNNY DAYS, SUNNY DAYS by Aileen Fisher. Copyright © 1958, 1986 by Aileen Fisher. "Horses" from UP THE WINDY HILL by Aileen Fisher. Copyright © 1953, 1981 Aileen Fisher. Both reprinted by permission of Marian Reiner for the author.

ROBERT FROST. "The Pasture" from THE POETRY OF ROBERT FROST, edited by Edward Connery Lathem. Copyright 1939, © 1967, 1969 by Henry Holt and Co. Reprinted by permission of Henry Holt and Company, Inc.

PATRICIA HUBBELL. "Grandmother's Garden Song" by Patricia Hubbell. Copyright © 2000 by Patricia Hubbell. Used by permission of Marian Reiner for the author.

JOY N. HULME. "Down on the Corn Farm" by Joy N. Hulme. Copyright © 2000 by Joy N. Hulme. Used by permission of the author.

SANDRA LIATSOS. "In the Chicken Coop" by Sandra Liatsos. Copyright © 2000 by Sandra Liatsos. By permission of Marian Reiner for the author. "On an Apple Farm" by Sandra Liatsos appeared originally in THE VINE. Copyright 1980 by Graded Press. Used by permission.

KRIS ARO McLEOD. "Fall Fields" by Kris Aro McLeod. Copyright © 2000 by Kris Aro McLeod. Used by permission of the author.

MICHIO MADO. "The Goats and the Letters" from THE MAGIC POCKET: Selected Poems by Michio Mado, translated by the Empress Michiko of Japan. English translation copyright © 1998 the Empress Michiko of Japan. Reprinted with the permission of Margaret K. McElderry Books, an imprint of Simon & Schuster Children's Publishing Division.

JOSÉ-LUIS OROZCO. "Five Little Chickies" and "Cinco Pollitos" from DIEZ DEDITOS TEN LITTLE FINGERS, Selected, Arranged, and Translated by Jose-Luis Orozco. Copyright © 1997 José-Luis Orozco. Used by permission of Dutton Children's Books, a division of Penguin Putnam, Inc.

ROBERT SCOTELLARO. "Farmer Pete" by Robert Scotellaro. Copyright © 2000 by Robert Scotellaro. Used by permission of the author.

KATIE McALLASTER WEAVER. "Seeds" by Katie McAllaster Weaver. Copyright © 2000 by Katie McAllaster Weaver. Used by permission of the author.

JANE YOLEN. "Shepherd's Night Count" from DRAGON NIGHT AND OTHER LULLABIES by Jane Yolen. Copyright © 1980 by Jane Yolen. Reprinted by permission of Curtis Brown, Ltd.

Scholastic Inc. grants teachers permission to photocopy the poems from this book for classroom use. No other part of this publication may be reproduced in whole or in part, or stored in a retrieval system, or transmitted in any form or by any means, electronic, mechanical, photocopying, recording, or otherwise, without permission of the publisher. For information regarding permission, write to Scholastic Professional Books, 555 Broadway, New York, NY 10012-3999.

Cover design by Norma Ortiz
Interior design by Ellen Hassell
for Boultinghouse & Boultinghouse, Inc.
Illustrations by Maxie Chambliss
Copyright © 2000 by Betsy Franco
ISBN: 0-439-09847-5
Printed in the U.S.A.

Contents

Introduction

This collection of poems and the other collections in this series will come in very handy as you dive into your yearly themes. The poetry in *On the Farm* has been thoughtfully written and compiled with preschool to second-grade children clearly in mind. Variety, usability, and fun topped the list of considerations in selecting or creating each and every poem.

There are so many ways the poems can be used, so why not get the most you can from each one? Whether you present a poem a week or a poem a day, you can dip into this collection with confidence. Use the poems in coordination with your phonics program. You can read aloud the poems, transfer them to the pocket chart, and then let children act them out. The collection provides jumping-off points for writing and fits into the science, math, and social studies curricula as well.

Phonemic Elements

Phonics and poetry go hand in hand. For instance, look at the rhyming words in the poem "Baby Chick" (page 16)—*peck, egg, neck, leg.* Transfer this eight-line poem to a pocket chart and then highlight the rhyming words. This can lead nicely into other activities that focus on the short-*e* sound.

Similarly, "The Barn Cats" (page 17) works well for the long-vowel sounds, and "I'm a Little Piglet" (page 19) is tailor-made for working on blends (*stout, snout, slop, stop*).

Some poems naturally lend themselves to consonant study. "Grandmother's Garden Song" (page 9) has several words that begin with the letter *p,* as does "Pink-Skinned Pigs" (page 19). Introduce the poem "Fall Fields" (page 11) to your class and use it to have fun with the letter *c.*

Being Authors and Illustrators

Predictable language in poetry can make children feel confident about their own reading and writing. Help children anticipate the rhyming words or repeated phrases in the poems. Then encourage them to go one step farther by making up new verses, or poems on similar themes or in similar formats. For instance, in "The Pasture" (page 18), Robert Frost invites the reader to join him in his activities, with the phrase "You come too." Children can write about chores or activities they would like to do on a farm and use Frost's phrase at the end. They can also have fun rewriting the even lines of "One, Two" (page 14). For example *moo* rhymes with *two,* and *pen* rhymes with *ten.*

A poem such as "Baa, Baa, Black Sheep" (page 24) can be duplicated on a page with appropriate blanks for children to complete, as shown below. They might try a goat (milk, cheese), a hen (eggs), and a cow (milk). In line 5, they can fill in their own names. Let children complete this activity individually or as a class.

_____, _____, _____,
Have you any _____?
Yes sir, yes sir,
Yes I do.
One for (name of child in class) ,
One for my dame,
And one for the little boy
who lives in the lane.

When a poem looks like what it's saying, as "What kind of apples?"(page 27) does, it is called a visual or concrete poem. Children can make their own visual poetry inside the shape of an apple. They might describe an apple with seeds or a worm inside. Or they might draw an apple with a bite out of it, and inside that shape, describe what it's like to eat an apple.

Some poems ask questions. The goats in "The Goats and the Letters" (page 21) ask each other, "What, by the way, did your letter say?" Children can use their imaginations to write the letters that were eaten by the goats.

Why not take a poem and make it into a little foldable book, with one line per page? Children can illustrate each page, making the poem more personal and, subsequently, more meaningful. A class collaborative book can be similarly effective. "The Mixed-Up Farm" (page 26) might spawn a silly book of farm animals making the wrong sounds and then the right sounds.

Reading and Acting Out Poetry

Poems provide delightful opportunities for dramatic play. Children can perform the suggested fingerplay that accompanies "Here Is the Barn" (page 8) or act out the poems "Baby Chick" (page 16) or "The Goats and the Letters" (page 21).

Some poems can be adapted to a call-and-response format in which half the class says some of the lines or verses and the other half completes the lines or verses. You can use "Barnyard Chat" (page 12) in this way and let children act it out as well. Poems such as "Baby Farm Animals" (page 11) and "Sheep on the Loose" (page 25) work well in a Reader's Theater format—different lines can be assigned to different children.

With many poems in the collection, it can be fun to emphasize the rhyme and rhythm as you read. Urge children to clap, snap, or jump to the rhythm so they can feel the poems in their bodies.

Science, Math, and Social Studies Links

Biology is inherent to a study of the farm. What a rich body of knowledge can be learned from poems about chicks hatching, baby animals, planting seeds, and farm animal behavior! Respect for nature's wonders is another lesson that reverberates throughout the collection.

Math opportunities abound as well. You can use the poem "One, Two" (page 14) for counting. After reading "Chook-Chook-Chook" (page 17), invite children to change the numbers in the poem and illustrate the results as an addition activity. "Pretty Little Rooster" (page 15) leads nicely into activities about time.

The collection includes multicultural selections that help children appreciate diverse cultures. For example, "Pretty Little Rooster" (page 15) is a traditional Chinese nursery rhyme translated and adapted from the Chinese. "Rudolph Is Tired of the City" (page 31) is written by the well-known African American poet, Gwendolyn Brooks.

The Home Connection

Poetry always works well as a link to the home. Children can share the poems, their illustrations of the poems, or new verses the class wrote. Poetry is short and easy to read, and it has emotional power for both children and their families.

The treasures in *On the Farm* are yours for the taking. Take advantage of the curricular links, the phonetics, the reading and writing opportunities, and the multicultural aspects— But most of all, enjoy the poetry!

A Farm Visit

My class went to a farm one day,
We touched the soft, brown cow.
We saw where all the milk came from—
I understand it now.

We stroked a chicken's feathers
and we touched a muddy pig.
Her hairs were like a bristly brush,
Her eyes weren't very big.

We watched the goats butt heads
and put their hooves up on the wall.
A little baby lamb was
with her mama in a stall.

We ate some carrots from the ground,
a fresh and healthy snack.
That farm was really neat—
I hope my class and I come back.

Betsy Franco

Thematic Poems for the Classroom: On the Farm   Scholastic Professional Books

Early Morning on the Farm

Waking at four
Milking the cows
Gathering eggs
warm from the hen.

Eating fresh eggs
Drinking sweet milk
Then cleaning and feeding
the pigs in their pen.

Betsy Franco

Chores

Digging carrots by the roots,
Counting piglets by their snoots,
Picking up the fallen fruits,
Best be sure to wear your boots.

Marcy Barack

Here Is the Barn

Here is the barn.
Open it wide.
Let's go inside
where the animals hide.

Here are the horses,
Here are the cows.
They're eating their dinner
and drinking right now.

They'll stay here till night
turns into the day.
When we open the doors,
they'll all mosey away.

Out in the pasture
they'll eat grass and hay.
The cows will moo softly.
The horses will neigh.

Betsy Franco

FINGERPLAY   *(similar to "Here is the church, here is the steeple . . .")*
1. Make a barn: interlace fingers of two hands inside palms, with thumbs as barn doors.
2. Open up barn by turning over hands to reveal finger horses and cows on each side.
3. Wiggle fingers to show cows and horses moving as they eat their food.
4. Unlink hands to open the barn doors.
5. Have finger cows and horses mosey away.
6. As animals eat in the pasture, raise fingertip heads to moo and neigh.

Thematic Poems for the Classroom: On the Farm Scholastic Professional Books

Grandmother's Garden Song

Carrots, onions,
Parsnips, kale—
If you'll come help me
We'll soon fill the pail.

Peas in the springtime,
Pumpkins in fall,
Beans in the summer—
Food for us all.

Patricia Hubbell

Oats and beans and barley grow,
Oats and beans and barley grow,
Do you or I or anyone know
how oats and beans and barley grow?

First the farmer sows his seed,
Then he stands and takes his ease,
Stamps his feet and claps his hands
And turns around to view the land.

Author Unknown

Down on the Corn Farm

When great-great-grandpa had a farm,
A hundred years ago,
The men and boys grew all the corn
And work went rather slow.

They turned the fertile furrows with
A plow behind a horse,
And dropped the seeds in one by one,
All by hand, of course.

Nowadays, on mama's farm
you'll see some different scenes.
My mama and her workers do
Their jobs on big machines.

The fields are leveled smooth as rugs
Across a hardwood floor,
And rows are plowed ten at a time,
Or sometimes even more.

The farming methods may have changed
As years have come and gone,
But some things still remain the same:
The sun comes up at dawn;

The ears sprout out and fatten up,
Are popped into a pot;
And corn is most delicious
When it's fresh and buttered hot.

Joy N. Hulme

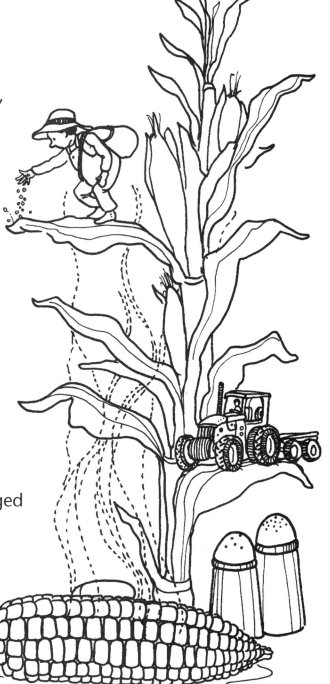
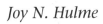

Thematic Poems for the Classroom: On the Farm   Scholastic Professional Books

Fall Fields

crows
stir up the air
over bare fields

caw, caw, caw
they say

crows fight
over a piece
of hard
corn

or a bit
of hay

Kris Aro McLeod

Baby Farm Animals

A baby horse is called a colt,
A calf's a baby cow.
A piglet is a baby pig,
A mama pig's a sow.

The goslings honk and run around,
The lambs turn into sheep.
The baby goats all kid around,
The kittens play and sleep.

I'm not sure what the farmer calls
a rooster when it's born,
or when it learns to doodle-doo
so early in the morn.

Betsy Franco

Thematic Poems for the Classroom: On the Farm   Scholastic Professional Books

Barnyard Chat

"Honk, honk."
"Oink, oink."
"Meow, meow."
"Neigh."

"Cluck, cluck."
"Woof, woof."
"Gobble, gobble."
"Bray!"

"Baa, baa."
"Hoot, hoot!"
"Cackle, cackle."
"Moo."

"Quack, quack."
"Peep, peep."
"Cock-a-doodle-doo!"

Stephanie Calmenson

Thematic Poems for the Classroom: On the Farm Scholastic Professional Books

Who's on the farm?

She guards her babies very well.
She nips at people walking by.
She hisses and she honk, honk, honks.
She waddles, swims, and even flies.

Who is she?   (goose)

He has a very wobbly chin.
His wings flap up and down.
Thanksgiving Day, he'd fly away
but he's stuck on the ground.

Who is he?   (turkey)

She chews her cud.
She softly moos.
Her fresh white milk's
her gift to you.

Who is she?   (cow)

Paddle, paddle, paddle,
Dive, dive, dive,
Quack, quack, quack.
It's good to be alive!

Who is he?   (duck)

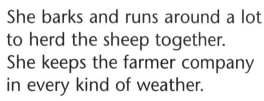

She barks and runs around a lot
to herd the sheep together.
She keeps the farmer company
in every kind of weather.

Who is she?   (sheep dog)

She hoots and hoots in the barn at night.
She catches lots of mice.
She turns her head this way and that
and blinks her two large eyes.

Who is she?   (barn owl)

Clippity clop, clippity clop.
He lifts his head to neigh.
He's trotting to the big red barn
to eat some fresh-cut hay.

Who is he?   (horse)

Betsy Franco

Thematic Poems for the Classroom: On the Farm   Scholastic Professional Books

One, Two

One, two,
    The horse needs a shoe.
Three, four,
    The pigs want more.
Five, six,
    Here come the chicks.
Seven, eight,
    Cows at the gate.
Nine, ten,
    A big, fat hen.

Betsy Franco

Thematic Poems for the Classroom: On the Farm Scholastic Professional Books

Pretty Little Rooster

At one o'clock the rooster sings,
At two o'clock he crows.
At 3 and 4, he tells the time.
At 5 he crows and then I know
I must get up and go.

*Chinese nursery rhyme
translated and adapted by
Betsy Franco and So-Ching Brazer*

In the Chicken Coop

The hens and the rooster
　　are huddled together
cramped in the coop
　　in the wintry weather,
cackling and clucking
　　and pecking each other.
I'm glad none of them
　　is my sister or brother.

Sandra Liatsos

Thematic Poems for the Classroom: On the Farm   Scholastic Professional Books

Baby Chick

Peck, peck, peck
on the warm brown egg.
Out comes a neck!
Out comes a leg!

How does a chick
who's not been about,
discover the trick
of how to get out?

Aileen Fisher

Five Little Chickies

Five little chickies
has my aunt Tamba.

One sings so pretty,

one says, "¡Caramba!"

And the three others
play a great samba!

*translated by
José-Luis Orozco*

Cinco Pollitos

Cinco pollitos
tiene mi tía.

Uno le canta,

otro le pía.

Y tres le tocan
la sinfonía.

*traditional rhyme
from Latin America*

Thematic Poems for the Classroom: On the Farm Scholastic Professional Books

Chook-Chook-Chook

Chook, chook, chook-chook-chook.
Good Morning, Mrs. Hen.
How many children have you got?
Madam, I've got ten.

Four of them
Are yellow,
And four of them
Are brown,
And two of them
Are speckled red—
The nicest in the town!

Author Unknown

The Barn Cats

In the cow barn
live the cats
who chase the mice
and catch the rats
and when they're done
they get a treat—
two bowls of cow milk,
warm and sweet.

Betsy Franco

Thematic Poems for the Classroom: On the Farm Scholastic Professional Books

Cows

This morning when the cows woke up,
we milked them in the barn.

The cow's my favorite one of
all the animals on the farm.

Right now they're in the pasture—
some brown, some white and black.

They swish their tails at all the flies
that land upon their backs.

They chew their cud and graze about.
Their eyes are big and kind.

I'm sitting on their pasture fence
and they don't seem to mind.

Betsy Franco

The Pasture

I'm going out to clean the pasture spring;
I'll only stop to rake the leaves away
(And wait to watch the water clear, I may):
I sha'n't be gone long.—You come too.

I'm going out to fetch the little calf
That's standing by the mother. It's so young
It totters when she licks it with her tongue.
I sha'n't be gone long.—You come too.

Robert Frost

Thematic Poems for the Classroom: On the Farm Scholastic Professional Books

I'm a Little Piglet

I'm a little piglet,
short and stout.
Here is my tail.
Here is my snout.
If another piglet
takes my slop,
I yank his ear
to make him stop.

Betsy Franco

Pink-Skinned Pigs

The pink-skinned pigs
roll in the mud
because it's not much fun
to get a piggy sunburn
in the blazing summer sun.

Betsy Franco

Thematic Poems for the Classroom: On the Farm   Scholastic Professional Books

Bingo

There was a farmer had a dog
and Bingo was his name-o.
B-I-N-G-O,
B-I-N-G-O,
B-I-N-G-O,
and Bingo was his name-o.

Author Unknown

Thematic Poems for the Classroom: On the Farm Scholastic Professional Books

The Goats and the Letters

Black Goat received White Goat's letter.
He ate it up before he read it.
"Oo-la-la! What shall I do?"
He wrote a letter asking:
"What, by the way, did your letter say?"

White Goat received Black Goat's letter.
He ate it up before he read it.
"Oo-la-la! What shall I do?"
He wrote a letter asking:
"What, by the way, did your letter say?"

written by Michio Mado,
translated by the Empress Michiko of Japan

Bella and Benny

We have two goats
with horns and beards.
They chew most anything—
like old tin cans
and table scraps
and bark and corn and beans.

Those silly goats
eat all day long.
They never get enough.
And when they play
they butt their heads
and act like they're so tough.

Betsy Franco

Thematic Poems for the Classroom: On the Farm   Scholastic Professional Books

Horses

Back and forth
and up and down
horses' tails go switching.

Up and down
and back and forth
horses' skins go twitching.

Horses do
a lot of work
to keep themselves from itching.

Aileen Fisher

Bathing Puddles

It rained last night,
The ground's all wet.
The cows leave puddles where they've been.

For ducks, those puddles
are just right
for quacking, splashing, bathing in.

Betsy Franco

Thematic Poems for the Classroom: On the Farm Scholastic Professional Books

Farmer Pete

Now Farmer Pete,
He liked things neat.
His chickens all wore suits.
He had his cats
Wear dainty hats,
And all his pigs wore boots.

Robert Scotellaro

Baa, Baa, Black Sheep

Baa, Baa, Black Sheep,
Have you any wool?
Yes sir, yes sir,
Three bags full.
One for my master,
One for my dame,
And one for the little boy
who lives in the lane.

Author Unknown

To Market

To market, to market,
To buy a fat pig;
Home again, home again,
Jiggety jig.

To market, to market,
To buy a fat hog;
Home again, home again,
Joggety jog.

Author Unknown

Thematic Poems for the Classroom: On the Farm　Scholastic Professional Books

Sheep on the Loose

"The sheep got loose,
The sheep got loose!"
loudly honked
the farmer's goose.

The chickens pecked
the sheep's thick wool,
the goats all pushed,
the ducks all pulled.

The rooster called
the sheepdog Jack
and sure enough,
Jack had the knack.
He made those silly sheep go back.

Betsy Franco

Thematic Poems for the Classroom: On the Farm   Scholastic Professional Books

woof!

The Mixed-Up Farm

The farm got
all mixed up one day.
The piglets mooed,
The sheep said, "Neigh."

The rooster barked
to ask for food,
The goats all cock-a-doodle-dooed!

The farmer worked
all day and night
to straighten out the farm again.

The pigs said, "Oink."
The horse said, "Neigh."
But "Moo, moo, moo," said mother hen.

Betsy Franco

Thematic Poems for the Classroom: On the Farm   Scholastic Professional Books

On an Apple Farm

It's time for apple cider,
And for roasted apples, too,
And taffy apples
Sitting on a stick.
I'd rather have October
Than April, May, or June,
For we've apples
By the bushel we can pick.

Sandra Liatsos

What kind of apples are sticky and crunchy and easy to hold in your

h
a
n
d
?

Betsy Franco

Thematic Poems for the Classroom: On the Farm   Scholastic Professional Books

Sitting on the Tractor

High in the tractor,
my dad waves to me.
He's plowed all the fields
and he's sowing the seed.

In fall in the thresher,
he'll harvest the grain.
In spring, he'll be plowing
the fields again.

Betsy Franco

Thematic Poems for the Classroom: On the Farm   Scholastic Professional Books

Pumpkin Patch

The sunlight hits the hillside where
the farmer's pumpkins grow.
They're bright, bright orange
with vines of green.
They're sitting out in rows.

Some big, some small, some weirdly shaped,
some rough, some smooth and round,
I pick my favorite of the bunch.
They weigh it by the pound.

When we get home, I'll scoop it out
and roast the pumpkin seeds.
I'll carve my jack-o-lantern's face.
How scary it will be!

Betsy Franco

Seeds

I'm waiting quite patiently.
Soon, I hope that I will see
something green peeking, showing,
baby bud sneaking, growing.
Tiny tips pry through the earth
I am sure it will be worth
such a wait. Soon I will know
what it's like to see seeds grow.

Katie McAllaster Weaver

Family Garden on the Farm

Corn and beans,
Corn and beans,
Silly scarecrows in between.
Cukes and lettuce,
Cukes and lettuce,
We can eat them when they let us.
Sweet green peas,
Sweet green peas,
Munch and crunch them, as we please!

Betsy Franco

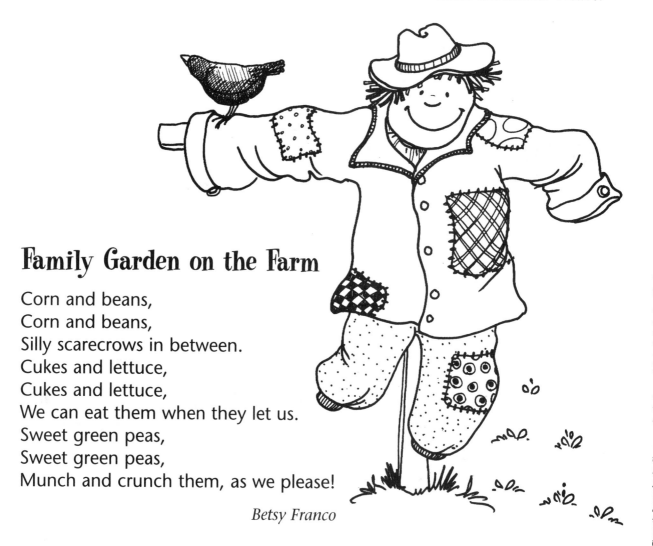

Thematic Poems for the Classroom: On the Farm Scholastic Professional Books

Thematic Poems for the Classroom: On the Farm   Scholastic Professional Books

Rudolph Is Tired of the City

These buildings are too close to me.
I'd like to PUSH away.
I'd like to live in the country,
And spread my arms all day.

I'd like to spread my breath out, too—
As farmers' sons and daughters do.

I'd tend the cows and chickens.
I'd do the other chores.
Then, all the hours left I'd go
A-SPREADING out-of-doors.

Gwendolyn Brooks

Shepherd's Night Count

One ewe,
one ram,
Two sheep,
One lamb,
Three sheep,
One flock,
Four gates,
One lock,
Five folds,
One light,
Good dog,
Good night.

Jane Yolen

Thematic Poems for the Classroom: On the Farm Scholastic Professional Books